一柳 慧

ピアノのための

雲の表情 X

TOSHI ICHIYANAGI
CLOUD ATLAS X

for piano

SJ 1122

SCHOTT

ピアノのための《雲の表情Ⅹ—雲・空間—》は、木村かをりの委嘱により、連作《雲の表情》の最終作品として作曲された。
1999年6月14日に、東京で、木村かをりにより初演された。

演奏時間—— 6分

Cloud Atlas Ⅹ -Cloud in the Space- for piano was commissioned by Kaori Kimura.
It was composed as the last work in the piano music cycle *Cloud Atlas.*

The first perfomance was given by Kaori Kimura in Tokyo on June 14, 1999.

Duration: 6 minutes

SYMBOLS:

◆   =Silent key (Depress the key silently and hold.)

       =Chromatic cluster

Mute   =Muted sound (Touch the string of the written note firmly and play the same note
        on the keyboard.)

Accidentals apply only to each note.

Cloud Atlas
雲の表情
X
Cloud in Space
雲・空間

Toshi Ichiyanagi

一柳 慧

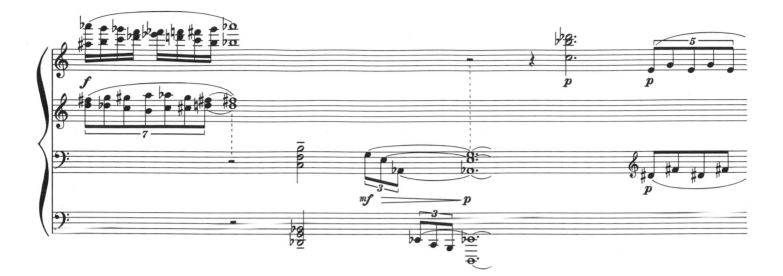

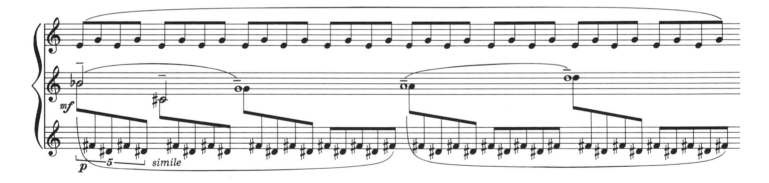

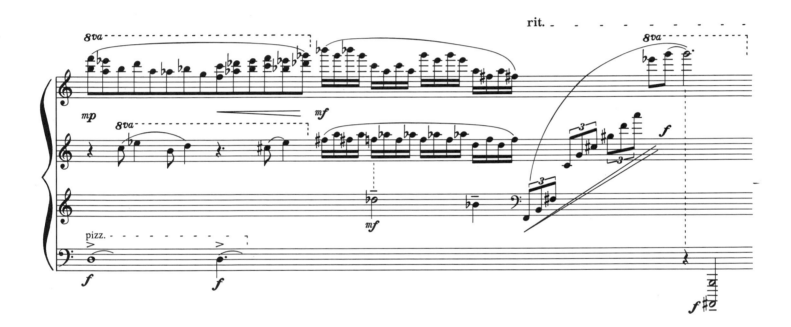

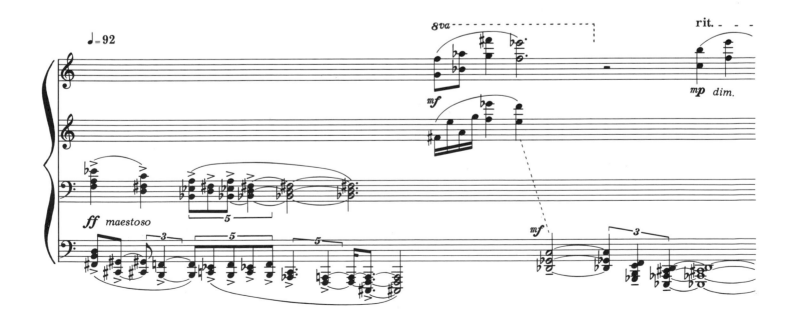

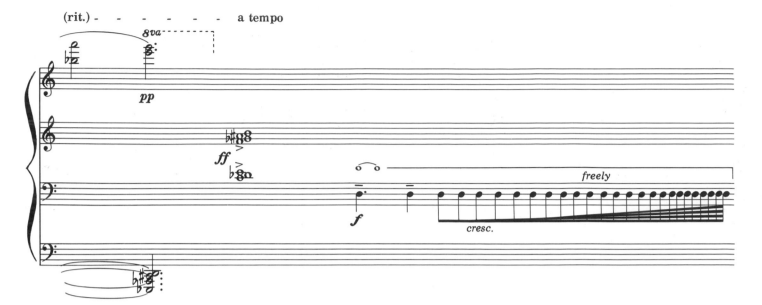

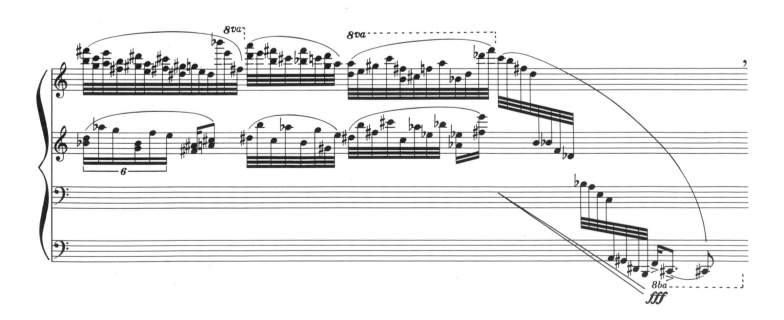

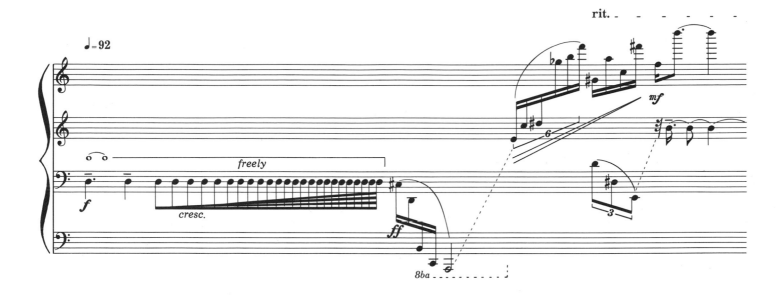

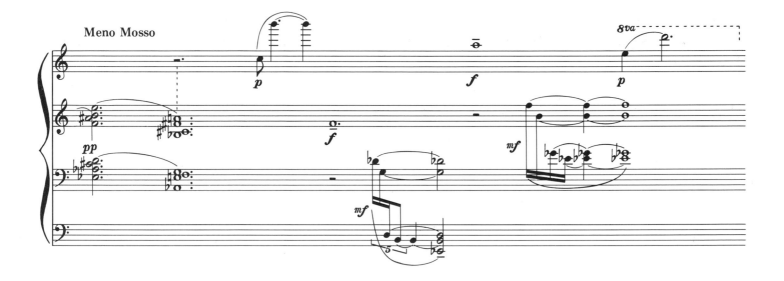

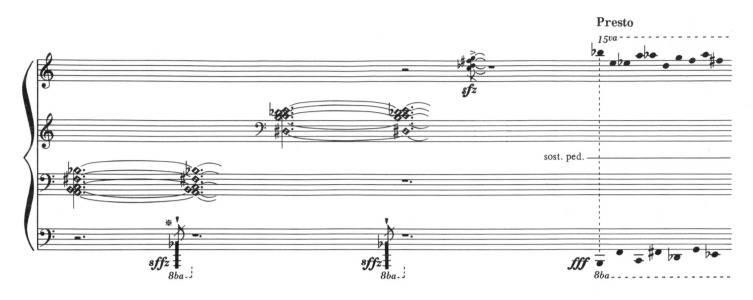

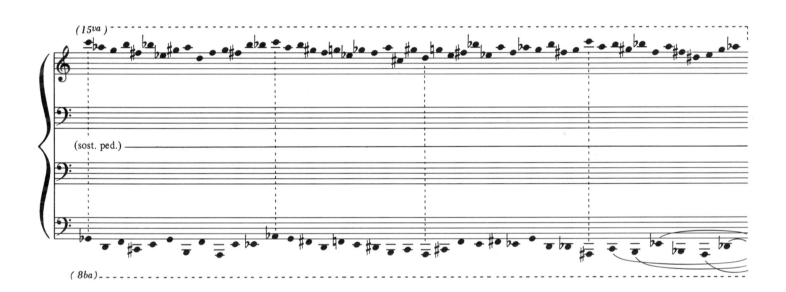

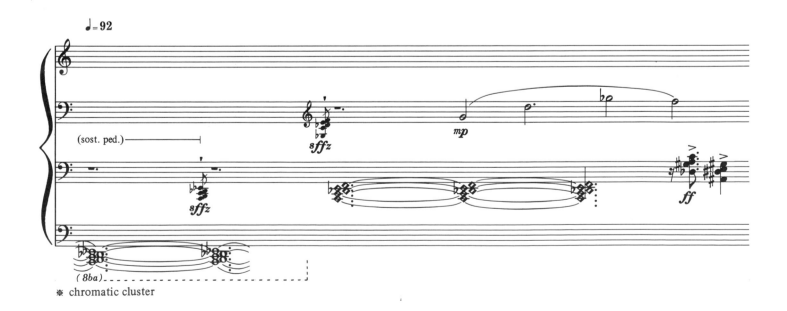

✻ chromatic cluster

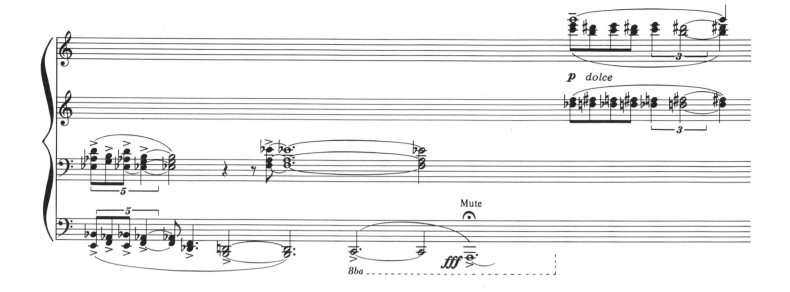

Meno Mosso

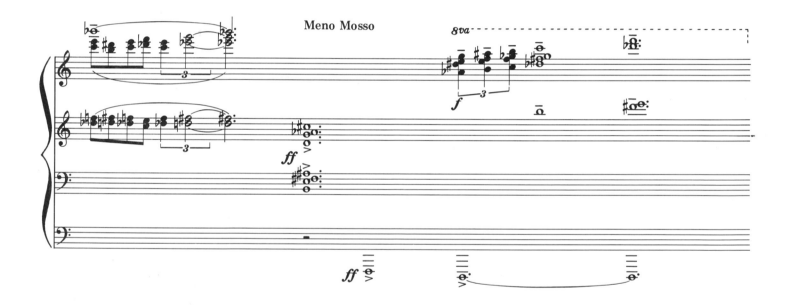

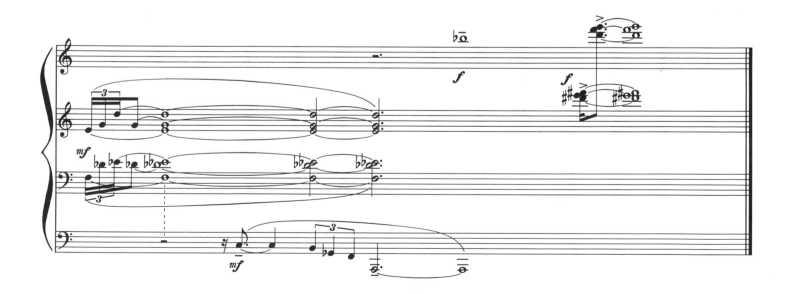

一柳　慧《雲の表情X》　　　　　　　　　　　●

初版発行—————————————————————2000年 4 月 3 日

発行———————————————————日本ショット株式会社

————————————————————東京都千代田区飯田橋2-9-3 かすがビル 2 階

————————————————————〒102-0072

————————————————————(03)3263-6530

————————————————————ISBN4-89066-422-X

————————————————————ISMN M-65001-166-2